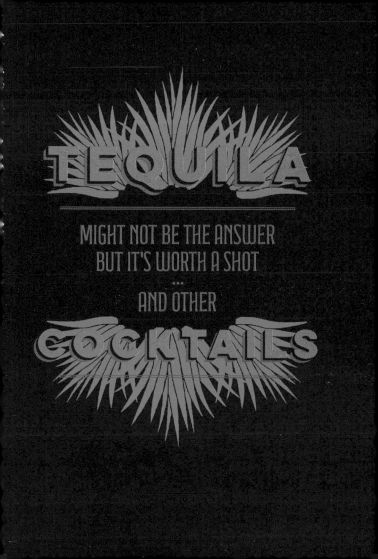

TEQUILA

MIGHT NOT BE THE ANSWER
BUT IT'S WORTH A SHOT
...
AND OTHER
COCKTAILS

An Hachette UK Company
www.hachette.co.uk

First published in Great Britain in 2023 by Godsfield,
an imprint of Octopus Publishing Group Ltd
Carmelite House, 50 Victoria Embankment, London EC4Y 0DZ
www.octopusbooks.co.uk

ISBN 978-1-7847-2937-0

A CIP catalogue record for this book is available from the British Library

Printed and bound in China

10 9 8 7 6 5 4 3 2 1

Publisher: Lucy Pessell
Designer: Isobel Platt
Editor: Feyi Oyesanya
Assistant Editor: Samina Rahman
Production Controller: Allison Gonsalves

Illustrations: Yelyzaveta Matiushenko/iStock

TEQUILA

MIGHT NOT BE THE ANSWER
BUT IT'S WORTH A SHOT
...
AND OTHER

COCKTAILS

60 TEQUILA & MEZCAL RECIPES

hamlyn

CONTENTS

MEASURES

The measure that has been used in the recipes is based on a bar jigger, which is 25 ml (1 fl oz).

If preferred, a different volume can be used, providing the proportions are kept constant within a drink and suitable adjustments are made to spoon measurements, where they occur.

Standard level spoon measurements are used in all recipes.

1 tablespoon = one 15 ml spoon (0.5 fl oz)
1 teaspoon = one 5 ml spoon (0.2 fl oz)

INTRODUCTION

All tequila is mezcal, but not all mezcal is tequila; mezcal is made from the agave plant but to be called tequila, it must be made from the Blue Agave, also known as the Maguey Agave.

We've collected over 60 recipes that let the agave spirit shine. There are well-known classics alongside fun twists and variations that won't fail to impress even the harshest of critics.

Tequila tends to be smoother and a touch spicier than smokier, earthier mezcal and we've recommended which spirit to use throughout the book but it's down to personal taste so mix away and find your favourite!

The cocktails are divided into categories of glass type, and the bar basics section will tell you everything you need to know before you get shaking.

SHOTS

DASH LOVE

2 teaspoons light crème de cacao
1 measure chilled tequila
2–3 drops raspberry purée

Pour the crème de cacao into a shot glass.

Using the back of a bar spoon, slowly float the chilled tequila over the crème de cacao.

Carefully add the raspberry purée to the surface of the liquid — it should sink and then float midway.

PASSION SPAWN

* works well with mezcal *

---

1 measure silver tequila
1 dash Triple Sec
1 dash lime juice
1 passion fruit

Add tequila, Triple Sec and lime juice to a shaker, fill with ice and shake hard.

Strain into a chilled shot glass.

Cut the passion fruit in half and squeeze the pulp over the shot before serving.

RASPBERRY BERET

½ measure light crème de cacao
1 measure chilled gold tequila
1 plump raspberry

Pour the crème de cacao into a shot glass.

Using the back of a bar spoon, slowly float
the tequila over the crème de cacao.

Slowly lower the raspberry into the drink –
it will settle between the two liquids.

TEQUILA SLAMMER

1 measure gold tequila
1 measure Champagne

Pour the tequila into a shot glass and slowly top with Champagne.

Cover the top of the glass with the palm of your hand to seal the contents inside and grip it with your fingers.

Briskly pick up the glass and slam it down on to a surface to make the drink fizz, then quickly gulp it down in one, while it is still fizzing.

MARGARITAS

COBALT
MARGARITA

---

1 lime wedge
fine sea salt
1 ½ measures tequila
2 teaspoons Cointreau
½ measure Blue Curaçao
¾ measure lime juice
¾ measure grapefruit juice
lime rind spiral, to garnish

Frost the rim of a chilled margarita glass
by moistening it with a lime wedge, then
pressing it into salt.

Add the tequila, Cointreau, Curaçao and
fruit juices to a shaker filled with ice and
shake vigorously for 10 seconds.

Strain into the prepared glass,
garnish and serve.

GRANDE MARGARITA

1 lime wedge
course sea salt
2 measures gold tequila
1 measure lime juice
1 measure Triple Sec
lime slice, to garnish

Frost the rim of a margarita glass by
moistening it with a lime wedge, then
pressing it into the salt.

Add the tequila, lime juice and Triple Sec to
a shaker filled with ice and shake hard.

Strain into the prepared glass,
garnish and serve.

PASSION FRUIT MARGARITA

lime wedge
coarse sea salt
1 ½ measures gold tequila
1 measure Cointreau
1 teaspoon passion fruit syrup
1 measure fresh lime juice
pulp and seeds of 1 passion fruit
mint sprig, to garnish

Frost the rim of a margarita glass by moistening it with a lime wedge, then pressing it into the salt.

Add tequila, Cointreau, passion fruit syrup, lime juice and half of the passion fruit to a shaker filled with ice and shake hard.

Double strain into the prepared glass, add the remaining passion fruit pulp, garnish and serve.

SOMBRERO

¾ measure gold tequila
¾ measure white crème de cacao
3 ½ measures single cream
grated nutmeg, to garnish

Add all ingredients to a shaker, fill with ice
and shake vigorously for 10 seconds.

Strain into a chilled margarita glass, sprinkle
with grated nutmeg and serve.

SLINGS & HURRICANES

ACAPULCO BLISS

¾ measure tequila
1 tablespoon Pisang
Ambon (banana liqueur)
2 teaspoons Galliano
¾ measure lemon juice
3 ½ measures passion fruit juice
¾ measure single cream
To garnish
lemon slices
pineapple wedge
mint sprig

Add all ingredients to a shaker, fill with ice
and shake vigorously.

Pour into a large sling glass, garnish
and serve.

BECKONING LADY

2 measures tequila
4 measures passion fruit juice
1–2 teaspoons Galliano
cocktail cherries, to garnish

Fill a hurricane or highball glass with the ice.

Using the back of a bar spoon, slowly add
the tequila and passion fruit juice and stir
well to mix.

Float the Galliano on top in a layer about 1
cm (half an inch) deep, garnish and serve.

BROOKLYN BOMBER

1 measure tequila
½ measure Cointreau
½ measure cherry brandy
½ measure Galliano
1 measure lemon juice
To garnish
orange slice
cocktail cherry

Add all ingredients to a shaker, fill with
ice and shake hard.

Strain into a hurricane glass filled with
crushed ice, garnish and serve with straws.

PLAYA DEL MAR

1 orange slice
light brown sugar and course sea
salt, mixed
1 ¼ measures gold tequila
¾ measure Grand Marnier
2 teaspoons lime juice
¾ measure cranberry juice
¾ measure pineapple juice
To garnish
pineapple wedge
orange rind spiral

Frost the rim of a sling glass by moistening
it with the orange slice, then pressing it
into the sugar and salt mixture.

Carefully fill the glass with ice.

Pour the tequila, Grand Marnier and fruit
juices into a shaker, fill with ice and
shake vigorously for 10 seconds.

Strain into the prepared glass, garnish
and serve.

TAHITIAN PEARL

2 measures 100 per cent agave
blanco tequila
1 measure lime juice
4 teaspoons agave syrup
1 tinned peach half, drained
2 measures cloudy apple juice
2 measures pineapple juice
1 teaspoon grenadine
5 mint leaves
To garnish
lime wheel
basil leaf

Add all ingredients to a food processor
or blender and blend until smooth.

Pour into a hurricane glass, garnish
and serve.

TIJUANA SLING

1 ¼ measures tequila
¾ measure crème de cassis
¾ measure lime juice
2 dashes Peychaud's bitters
3 ½ measures dry ginger ale
To garnish
lime slice
blackcurrants or blueberries

Add the tequila, crème de cassis, lime juice and bitters to a shaker, fill with ice and shake vigorously.

Pour into a large sling glass full of ice and top with ginger ale.

Garnish and serve.

HIGHBALLS
& COLLINS

AGAVE JULEP

* works well with mezcal *

---

8 mint leaves, torn
1 tablespoon sugar syrup
1 ¼ measures gold tequila
1 ¼ measures lime juice
To garnish
lime wedge
mint sprig

Muddle the mint leaves with the sugar syrup
in a highball glass.

Add the tequila and lime juice, fill the glass
with crushed ice and stir vigorously to mix.

Garnish and serve.

ALLELUIA

¾ measure tequila
½ measure Blue Curaçao
2 teaspoons maraschino syrup
1 dash egg white
¾ measure lemon juice
3 ½ measures bitter lemon

To garnish
lemon slice
cocktail cherry
mint sprig

Pour the tequila, Curaçao, maraschino
syrup, egg white and lemon juice to a shaker,
fill with ice and shake vigorously.

Strain into a tall glass filled with ice, top with
the bitter lemon and stir gently.

Garnish and serve.

BATANGA

---

1 lime
course sea salt
2 measures Tequileño Blanco tequila
Mexican cola

Frost the rim of an old-fashioned glass
by moistening it with a lime wedge, then
pressing it into the salt.

Fill the glass with ice and add the tequila.

Squeeze half of the lime juice into the drink,
then gently stir and top with Mexican cola.

BORDER CROSSING

1 ½ measures gold tequila
1 measure lime juice
1 measure clear honey
4 dashes orange bitters
3 measures dry ginger ale
To garnish
blueberries
lime wedge

Add the tequila, lime juice, honey
and orange bitters to a shaker, fill with ice
and shake hard.

Pour into a highball glass, filled with ice
and top with ginger ale.

Garnish and serve.

EL DIABLO

* works well with mezcal *

---

1 ¼ measures tequila gold
¾ measure lime juice
2 teaspoons grenadine
3 ½ measures dry ginger ale

Fill a large highball glass with ice and add
the tequila, lime juice and grenadine.

Top with ginger ale and stir gently.

Garnish and serve.

JALISCO SWIZZLE

3 dashes Angostura bitters
¾ measure gold tequila
¾ measure golden rum
1 ½ measures lime juice
¾ measure passion fruit juice
2 teaspoons sugar syrup
soda water
To garnish
lime slice
mint sprig

Add the bitters, tequila, rum, fruit juices
and sugar syrup to a shaker, fill with ice and
shake vigorously for 10 seconds.

Strain into a highball glass filled with
crushed ice.

Top with soda water and stir briefly until a
frost forms.

Garnish and serve.

LONG ISLAND ICE TEA

½ measure vodka
½ measure gin
½ measure white rum
½ measure tequila
½ measure Cointreau
½ measure lemon juice
cola
lemon slice, to garnish

Add the vodka, gin, rum, tequila, Cointreau and lemon juice to a shaker, fill with ice and shake hard.

Strain into a highball glass filled with ice and top with cola.

Garnish and serve.

LOS ALTOS

5 slices tangerine
3 teaspoons agave syrup
2 measures tequila
2 teaspoons lime juice
2 teaspoons Campari
4 measures soda water
To garnish
orange slice
lime wedge

Add the tangerine slices and agave syrup
to a shaker and muddle.

Pour in the tequila, lime juice and Campari
and shake.

Strain into a glass filled with ice and top with
soda water, garnish and serve.

LUCHA LIBRE

2 measures each blanco tequila
cola
soda water
½ measure Triple Sec
½ lime juice
2 dashes orange bitters
lime wedges, to garnish

Fill a highball glass with ice and
add all ingredients.

Stir the mix, garnish and serve with a straw.

MEXICAN BULLDOG

¾ measure tequila
¾ measure Kahlúa
1 ¼ measures single cream
3 ½ measures cola
drinking chocolate powder, to garnish

Add the tequila, Kahlúa and cream to
a highball glass filled with ice, then top
with cola.

Stir gently, then sprinkle with the drinking
chocolate powder and serve.

MEXICAN MULE

works well with mezcal

---

1 lime
1 dash sugar syrup
1 measure José Cuervo gold tequila
1 measure Kahlúa
dry ginger ale

Cut the lime into slices, add them to
a highball glass and muddle together with
sugar syrup.

Half-fill the glass with crushed ice,
add the tequila and Kahlúa.

Stir the contents, then top with
ginger ale and serve.

MEXICANA

1 ¼ measures tequila
¾ measure framboise liqueur
¾ measure lemon juice
3 ½ measures pineapple juice
To garnish
pineapple wedge
lemon slice

Add all ingredients to a shaker, fill with ice
and shake vigorously for 10 seconds.

Strain into a large highball glass filled with
ice, garnish and serve.

MEXICOLA

4 lime wedges
1 ¼ measures tequila
6 measures cola

Muddle the lime wedges in a highball glass.

Fill the glass with crushed ice, then add the tequila and cola.

Stir gently, lifting the lime wedges through the drink, and serve.

PALOMA

½ pink grapefruit
2 measures blanco tequila
2 measures soda water
1 teaspoon agave syrup
pink grapefruit wedge, to garnish

Juice the pink grapefruit and add the juice
to a collins glass full of ice.

Add the remaining ingredients to the
glass and stir the mix.

Garnish and serve.

ROSARITA BAY BREEZE

---

1 ¼ measures tequila
6 measures cranberry juice
1 ½ measures pineapple juice
orange slice, to garnish

Add the tequila and cranberry juice to
a highball glass filled with ice and stir.

Float the pineapple juice on top, garnish
and serve.

SOUTH FOR THE SUMMER

works well with mezcal

---

2 teaspoons grenadine
2 measures tequila
3 measures orange juice
4 pineapple chunks
To garnish
pineapple leaf
orange rind

Spoon the grenadine into a highball glass.

Add crushed ice into a food processor or blender with the tequila, orange juice and pineapple chunks, and blend until smooth.

Pour the mixture over the grenadine, stir, garnish and serve.

SUNBURN

¾ measure gold tequila
1 tablespoon Cointreau
6 measures cranberry juice
orange slice, to garnish

Add all ingredients to a large highball glass
filled with ice and stir.

Garnish and serve.

TEQUILA DE COCO

1 measure tequila
1 measure lemon juice
1 measure coconut syrup
3 dashes maraschino liqueur
lemon slice, to garnish

Add all ingredients to a food processor or
blender with crushed ice. and blend for
a few seconds.

Pour into a collins glass, garnish and serve.

TEQUILA SUNRISE

2 measures tequila
4 measures orange juice
2 teaspoons grenadine
To garnish
orange slices
cocktail cherry

Add the tequila and orange juice to a shaker,
fill with ice and shake hard.

Strain into a highball glass filled with ice, top
with grenadine and allow it to sink
to the bottom of the glass, creating
a layered effect.

Garnish and serve.

TIJUANA MARY

4 chunks watermelon
2 measures tequila
2 teaspoons sriracha sauce
1 pinch course sea salt
2 pinches pink peppercorns
4 measures tomato juice
watermelon wedge, to garnish

Add the watermelon chunks to a
shaker and muddle.

Add the tequila, sriracha sauce, salt,
and peppercorns, fill the shaker with ice
and shake hard.

Strain into a glass filled with ice and top
with tomato juice.

Stir well, garnish and serve.

OLD
FASHIONEDS

BRAVE BULL

1 measure tequila
1 measure Kahlúa

Fill an old-fashioned glass with ice.

Add the tequila, Kahlúa and stir until
suitably chilled and serve.

DESERT DAISY

1 measure tequila
1 ¼ measures lime juice
2 teaspoons sugar syrup
1 tablespoon Fraise De Bois
To garnish
blackberry and strawberry
lime and orange wedges
mint sprig

Half-fill a large old-fashioned glass
with crushed ice.

Add the tequila, lime juice and sugar syrup,
and stir gently until a frost forms.

Add more crushed ice, then float the
Fraise de Bois on top.

Garnish and serve.

FOREST FRUIT

1 lime wedge
soft brown sugar
2 blackberries
2 raspberries
2 teaspoons Chambord
2 teaspoons crème de mûre
1 ¼ measures tequila
2 teaspoons Cointreau
1 ¼ measures lemon juice
To garnish
blackberries and raspberries
lemon slice

Rub the rim of a chilled old-fashioned glass
with a lime wedge and dip it in sugar.

In the glass, muddle the blackberries
and raspberries to a pulp, and stir in the
Chambord and crème de mûre.

Add the tequila, Cointreau and lemon juice,
fill with crushed ice and stir gently, lifting
the muddled berries through the drink.

Garnish and serve.

OLD-FASHIONED AT DUSK

2 measures tequila
2 teaspoons Islay whisky
1 teaspoon agave syrup
2 dashes Angostura bitters
orange twist, to garnish

Half-fill an old-fashioned glass with ice.

Add the ingredients to the glass and stir
for 1 minute.

Top with more ice, garnish
and serve.

PINK CADILLAC CONVERTIBLE

3 lime wedges
fine sea salt
1 ¼ measures gold tequila
½ measure cranberry juice
¾ measure Grand Marnier
lime wedge, to garnish

Frost the rim of a large old-fashioned glass by moistening it with a lime wedge, and press it into the salt.

Fill the glass with ice, and squeeze the juice from the remaining lime wedges to a shaker, pressing the rind to release its oils, then drop the wedges in.

Add tequila, cranberry juice and ice, and shake vigorously for 10 seconds, then strain into the prepared glass.

Drizzle Grand Marnier over the top, garnish and serve.

PRIMERA

1 ½ measures tequila
4 teaspoons Aperol
2 teaspoons sweet vermouth
3 teaspoons dry vermouth
2 dashes orange bitters
orange wedge, to garnish

Fill an old-fashioned glass with ice,
add all ingredients to the glass and stir.

Garnish and serve.

RUBY RITA

1 ¼ measures pink grapefruit juice
fine sea salt
1 ¼ measures gold tequila
¾ measure Cointreau
pink grapefruit wedge, to garnish

Frost the rim of an old-fashioned glass
by moistening it with some of the pink
grapefruit juice, then pressing it into
the salt.

Fill the glass with ice.

Add the tequila, Cointreau and the
remaining pink grapefruit juice to a shaker,
fill it with ice and shake vigorously.

Strain into the prepared glass,
garnish and serve.

WATERMELON SMASH

1 measure tequila
4 chunks watermelon
5 mint leaves
1 teaspoon agave syrup
mint sprig, to garnish

Add all the ingredients to a food processor
or blender and blend until smooth.

Pour into an old-fashioned glass,
garnish and serve.

COCKTAILS

BAJA SOUR

* works well with mezcal *

---

1 ¼ measures gold tequila
2 teaspoons sugar syrup
1 ¼ measures lemon juice
2 dashes orange bitters
½ egg white
1 tablespoon amontillado sherry
To garnish
lemon slices
orange rind spiral

Add the tequila, sugar syrup, lemon juice, bitters and egg white to a shaker filled with ice, and shake vigorously.

Pour into a large sour glass and drizzle the sherry over the drink.

Garnish and serve.

CADILLAC

---

3 lime wedges
fine sea salt
1 ½ measures gold tequila
½ measure Cointreau
1 ¼ measures lime juice
2 teaspoons Grand Marnier
lime slice, to garnish

Frost the rim of a chilled cocktail glass by
moistening it with a lime wedge,
then pressing it into the salt.

Add the tequila, Cointreau and lime juice
to a shaker filled with ice.

Squeeze the juice from the remaining
lime wedges into the shaker, pressing the
rind to release its oils, drop the wedges in,
and shake vigorously.

Strain into the prepared glass,
garnish and serve.

DIRTY SANCHEZ

2 teaspoons Noilly Prat vermouth
2 measures gold tequila
(preferably añejo)
2 teaspoons brine from a jar of
black olives
black olives, to garnish

Add vermouth to a mixing glass
filled with ice.

Stir to coat the ice, then discard the
excess vermouth.

Add the tequila and brine, and stir until
thoroughly chilled.

Strain into a chilled cocktail glass, garnish
with 2 black olives impaled on a cocktail
stick and serve.

FROSTBITE

1 measure tequila
1 measure double cream
1 measure white crème de cacao
½ measure white crème de menthe
drinking chocolate powder, to garnish

Add all ingredients to a shaker, fill with ice
and shake vigorously for 10 seconds.

Strain into a chilled cocktail glass.

Sprinkle with drinking chocolate powder
and serve.

HONEY WATER

1 ¼ measures gold tequila
¾ measure sweet vermouth
3 dashes Angostura bitters
3 dashes Peychaud's bitters
2 teaspoons Grand Marnier
To garnish
cocktail cherry
orange rind spiral

Add the tequila, vermouth and bitters to
a mixing glass filled with ice, and stir gently
for 10 seconds.

Pour Grand Marnier into a chilled cocktail
glass, swirl it round to coat the inside of the
glass, then tip it out.

Stir the contents of the mixing glass again
for 10 seconds.

Strain into the cocktail glass,
garnish and serve.

MARACUJA

* works well with mezcal *

---

1 fresh ripe passion fruit
1 ¼ measures gold tequila
1 tablespoon Créole Shrubb
¾ measure lime juice
2 teaspoons Cointreau
1 teaspoon passion fruit syrup
physalis (cape gooseberry), to garnish

Cut the passion fruit in half and scoop
the flesh into a shaker.

Add ice, tequila, Créole Shrubb, lime juice,
Cointreau and passion fruit syrup and shake
vigorously for 10 seconds.

Strain through a fine sieve into a chilled
cocktail glass, garnish and serve.

MOCKINGBIRD

1 ¼ measures tequila
¾ measure green crème de menthe
1 ¼ measures lime juice
lemon rind spiral, to garnish

Add all ingredients to a shaker filled with ice
and shake vigorously for about 10 seconds.

Strain into a chilled cocktail glass,
garnish and serve.

PALE ORIGINAL

2 measures gold tequila
½ measure ginger syrup
½ measure lime juice
1 measure guava juice
lime wedges, to garnish

Add all ingredients to a shaker, fill with ice
and shake hard.

Strain into a chilled cocktail glass,
garnish and serve.

PANCHO VILLA

1 measure tequila
½ measure Tia Maria
1 teaspoon Cointreau

Add all ingredients to a shaker, fill with ice
and shake vigorously until a frost forms.

Strain into a chilled cocktail glass and serve.

RUDE
COSMOPOLITAN

works well with mezcal

---

1 ½ measures gold tequila
1 measure Cointreau
1 measure cranberry juice
½ measure lime juice
lime wedge dusted in cocoa powder,
to garnish

Add all ingredients to a shaker, fill with ice
and shake vigorously for about 10 seconds.

Strain into a chilled Martini glass,
garnish with a lime wedge dusted
in cocoa powder and serve.

SILK STOCKING

drinking chocolate powder
¾ measure tequila
¾ measure white crème de cacao
3 ½ measures single cream
2 teaspoons grenadine

Frost the rim of a chilled cocktail glass by
dipping it into water, then pressing it into
the drinking chocolate powder.

Add the tequila, crème de cacao, cream
and grenadine to a shaker filled with ice,
and shake vigorously for 10 seconds.

Strain the drink into the prepared
glass and serve.

SOUR APPLE

1 ¼ measures tequila
2 teaspoons Cointreau
1 tablespoon apple schnapps
¾ measure lime juice
¾ measure unsweetened apple juice
granny smith apple wedge, to garnish

Add all ingredients to a shaker, fill with ice
and shake vigorously for about 10 seconds.

Strain into a chilled cocktail glass,
garnish and serve.

SOUTH OF THE BORDER

* works well with mezcal *

---

1 ¼ measures tequila
¾ measure Kahlúa
1 ¼ measures lime juice

Add all ingredients to a shaker, fill with ice and shake vigorously for about 10 seconds.

Strain the drink into a chilled cocktail glass and serve.

TEQUINI

3 dashes orange bitters
3 measures tequila blanco
2 teaspoons Noilly Prat
black olive, to garnish

Add bitters and tequila to a mixing glass
filled with ice, and stir gently for 10 seconds.

Pour vermouth into a chilled cocktail glass
and swirl to coat the inside, then tip it out.

Stir the bitters and tequila for a further
10 seconds and strain into the cocktail glass.

Garnish and serve.

THIGH HIGH

3 strawberries, hulled
1 teaspoon strawberry syrup
1 measure tequila
1 measure dark crème de cacao
1 ½ measures single cream
1 strawberry dipped in cocoa powder,
to garnish

Muddle the strawberries and strawberry
syrup in a shaker.

Add ice, tequila, crème de cacao, cream
and shake hard.

Strain into a large, chilled cocktail glass,
garnish and serve.

VIVA MARIA

1 measure tequila
½ measure lime juice
¼ measure maraschino liqueur
½ teaspoon grenadine
½ egg white
To garnish
lemon and lime slices
cocktail cherry

Add all ingredients to a shaker, fill with ice
and shake vigorously for about 10 seconds.

Strain into a cocktail glass filled with crushed
ice, garnish and serve.

MEZCAL

BLOODY MARY

2 measures mezcal
4 measures tomato juice
½ measure lemon juice
½ tablespoon fresh grated horseradish,
to taste
4 dashes Worcestershire sauce
3 dashes Tabasco sauce, to taste
1 pinch celery salt
1 pinch ground black pepper
To garnish
lime wedge, to garnish
cucumber spear, to garnish
½ jalapeño, to garnish

Add all ingredients to a shaker, fill with
ice and shake hard.

Strain into a tall glass filled with ice,
garnish and serve.

FRESH
PEACH SMASH

2 measures mezcal
½ fresh peach, pitted and skinned
1 teaspoon agave nectar
3 dashes Angostura bitters
1 slice fresh peach, to garnish

In a mixing glass muddle the peach until
most of the juice has been extracted and
strain into a shaker.

Add ice, mezcal, agave nectar, and bitters to
the shaker and shake until a frost forms.

Strain into a chilled coupe,
garnish and serve.

MANHATTAN

2 measures mezcal
1 measure sweet vermouth
3 dashes orange bitters
maraschino cherry, to garnish

Add all ingredients to a shaker, fill with ice
and stir continuously for 30 seconds.

Strain into a coupe, garnish and serve.

NAKED AND FAMOUS

1 measure mezcal
1 measure yellow or green Chartreuse
1 measure Aperol
1 measure fresh lime juice
1 lime wedge, to garnish

Add all ingredients to a shaker, fill with ice
and shake until a frost forms.

Strain into a coupe, garnish and serve.

MEZCAL NEGRONI

1 measure mezcal
2 tablespoons sweet red vermouth
1 measure Campari
orange peel, to garnish

Add all ingredients to a mixing glass
filled with ice and stir continuously
for 30 seconds.

Add ice to an old-fashioned glass,
and strain into the glass.

Cut a wide strip of the orange peel and
squeeze the orange peel into the drink to
release the oils.

Gently run the peel around the edge of the
glass, place into the glass
and serve.

OAXACA
OLD FASHIONED

---

1 measure tequila reposado
1 measure mezcal
1 teaspoon agave syrup
3 dashes chocolate bitters
orange peel, to garnish

Add all ingredients to a mixing glass
filled with ice and stir continuously
for 30 seconds.

Strain into an old-fashioned glass,
over a large ice cube.

Squeeze the oil of an orange peel over the
glass, place into the glass
and serve.

PALOMA

1 grapefruit wedge
flaky sea salt
1 measure tequila blanco
1 measure mezcal
4 tablespoons fresh grapefruit juice
1 tablespoon fresh squeezed lime juice
1 tablespoon simple syrup
2 measures soda water
grapefruit wedge, to garnish

Frost the rim of a chilled collins glass by
moistening it with a grapefruit wedge, then
pressing it into the salt.

Add the tequila, mezcal, grapefruit juice,
lime juice, syrup to the glass and stir.

Fill the glass with ice and top with soda
water, garnish and serve.

STRAWBERRY MEZCAL MOJITO

5 mint leaves
2 halved strawberries, tops removed
1 measure lime juice
½ measure agave
2 measures mezcal
soda water
To garnish
strawberries
mint sprig

Muddle the mint, strawberry, lime juice, and agave in a shaker.

Add mezcal and ice, and shake hard.

Pour contents into highball glass and top with fresh crushed ice, and finish with a splash of soda water.

Garnish and serve.

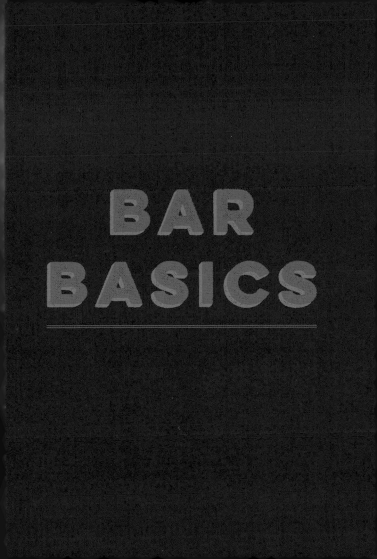

BAR
BASICS

WHAT MAKES A GOOD COCKTAIL?

Good cocktails, like good food, are based around quality ingredients. As with cooking, using fresh and homemade ingredients can often make the huge difference between a good drink and an outstanding drink. All of this can be found in department stores, online or in kitchen shops.

Ice
You'll need lots of it! Purchase good quality clear ice (the bigger the cubes, the better). If you're hosting a big party, it may be worthwhile finding if you have a local ice supplier that supplies catering companies, as this can be much more cost-effective.

Citrus juice
It's important to use fresh citrus juice in your drinks. Store your fruit out of the refrigerator at room temperature. Look for a soft-skinned fruit for juicing, which you can do with a juicer or citrus press. You can keep fresh citrus juice for a couple of days in the refrigerator, sealed to prevent oxidation.

Sugar syrup

You can buy sugar syrup or you can make your own. The most basic form of sugar syrup is made by mixing caster sugar and hot water together, and stirring until the sugar has dissolved. The key when preparing sugar syrups is to use a 1:1 ratio of sugar to liquid. White sugar acts as a flavour enhancer, while dark sugars have unique, more toffee flavours and work well with dark spirits.

Basic sugar syrup recipe
(Makes 1 litre (1¾ pints) of sugar syrup)

1. Dissolve 1 kg (2 lb) caster sugar in 1 litre (1¾ pints) of hot water.

2. Allow to cool.

Sugar syrup will keep in a sterilized bottle stored in the refrigerator for up to two weeks.

USEFUL EQUIPMENT

Shaker
The Boston shaker is the most simple option, but it needs to be used in conjunction with a Hawthorne strainer. Alternatively you could choose a shaker with a built-in strainer.

Hawthorne strainer
This type of strainer is often used in conjunction with a Boston shaker, but a simple tea strainer will also work well.

Measure or jigger
Single and double measures are available and are essential when you are mixing ingredients so that the proportions are always the same. One measure is 25 ml or 1 fl oz.

Mixing glass
A mixing glass is used for those drinks that require only a gentle stirring before they are poured or strained.

Bar spoon
Similar to a teaspoon but with a long handle, a bar spoon is used for stirring, layering and muddling drinks.

Muddling stick
Similar to a pestle, which will work just as well, a muddling stick, or muddler, is used to crush fruit or herbs in a glass or shaker for drinks like the Mojito.

Food processor
A food processor or blender is useful for making frozen cocktails and smoothies.

TECHNIQUES

Shaking
Shaking mixes ingredients thoroughly and quickly, and chills the drink before serving.

1. Fill a cocktail shaker with ice cubes, or cracked or crushed ice.

2. If the recipe calls for a chilled glass add a few ice cubes and some cold water to the glass, swirl it around and discard.

3. Add the ingredients to the shaker and shake until a frost forms on the outside.

4. Strain the cocktail into the glass and then serve.

Stirring

Stirring mixes and chills drinks, but also maintains their clarity.

1. Add the ingredients to a glass, in recipe order.
2. Use a bar spoon to stir the drink, lightly or vigorously, as described in the recipe.
3. Finish the drink with any decoration and serve.

Double-straining

To prevent all traces of puréed fruit and ice fragments from entering the glass, use a shaker with a built-in strainer in conjunction with a hawthorne strainer. A fine strainer also works well.

Muddling

A technique used to bring out the flavours of herbs and fruit using a blunt tool called a muddler.

1. Add chosen herb(s) to a highball glass. Add some sugar syrup and some lime wedges.

2. Hold the glass firmly and use a muddler or pestle to twist and press down.

3. Continue for 30 seconds, top up with crushed ice and add remaining ingredients.

Blending

Be careful not to add too much ice as this will dilute the cocktail. It's best to add a little at a time.

Layering

Some spirits can be served layered on top of each other – the more viscous or sugary the liquid, the heavier it will be.

1. Pour the heaviest liquid into a glass, taking care that it does not touch the sides.

2. Position a bar spoon in the centre of the glass, rounded part down and facing you. Rest the spoon against the side of the glass as your pour the next heaviest ingredient down the spoon. It should float on top of the first liquid.

3. Follow step 2, with the lightest ingredient at the top.